Prescription
of Civilization

문명의 처방전

English and Korean

Wansoo Kim

Korean Bestselling Author

ISBN-13: 978-1-946460-09-7

Library of Congress Control Number : 2019931232

Printed in the United States of America

Transcendent Zero Press

16429 El Camino Real Apt. #7

Houston, TX 77062

FIRST EDITION

Prescription
of Civilization

문명의 처방전

English and Korean

Wansoo Kim

Korean Bestselling Author

Preface

Preparing for the national exam for a diplomat while in university, I was extremely frustrated by the diagnosis that even modern medicine had no cure for my disease from the doctor at the best hospital in South Korea.

Finally I took a year off from university, went to my country home and struggled against disease being seriously tormented by the problems such as 'why on earth does such fatal disease come to me?, what will happen to me after death? etc.'

Attempting suicide a few times due to the unbearable pain, I had the opportunity to meet God at the revival service of a neighboring church. Beginning a life of faith, I've got a challenging hope of life with the miraculous healing of my disease. Besides, forming the sense of value totally different from that before the incurable disease, I have opened the eye of a new vision on everything of life.

Entering a graduate school and majoring in English and American poetry after graduating from university thanks to the recovery of health, I began to write poems, fired with the strong desire to express my literary and philosophical insight formed by the wide knowledge of English and American literature and the Christian faith.

My main concern was to diagnose the disease of modern civilization and find its solution through art(its possibility and limitation) and God(His completeness). It was because I realized keenly the distorted values and the structural injustice in society at large had been ingrainedly widespread, bumped against the wall of the irrational reality attempting to get a job for a professor for lots of years.

I have been writing poems in South Korea for more than 20 years. But I have decided to publish my book of poetry in America as I began the activity at a few poetry sites on the Internet at the beginning of last year. I hope, through this poetry book, the readers of the countries across the world who live a difficult life in the diseased modern civilization will find the prescription of consolation and healing.

Wansoo Kim November 1, 2018

서문 (Preface)

대학 시절 외교관이 되기 위한 국가고시를 준비하던 중, 한국 최고의 병원 의사로부터 내 병은 현대의학으로도 치료법이 없다는 진단을 받고 극심한 좌절을 했었다.

결국 휴학을 하고 시골에 있는 집에 가서, '왜 하필이면 나에게 이런 몹쓸 병이 찾아왔을까? 죽음 후에 나는 어찌 될까?' 등의 문제로 심각하게 가슴앓이를 하며 처절한 투병 생활을 하게 되었다.

견디기 힘든 고통으로 수차례 자살 기도를 하던 중, 이웃에 있는 교회의 집회에서 하나님을 만나는 기회를 얻었다. 신앙생활을 시작하며 질병의 기적적인 치유로 삶에 대한 도전적인 희망이 솟아났다. 게다가 난치병 이전과는 완전히 다른 가치관이 형성되며, 삶의 모든 것에 대한 새로운 비전의 눈을 뜨게 되었다.

건강의 회복으로 대학을 졸업한 후, 대학원에 진학하여 영미시를 전공하며, 영미문학의 폭넓은 지식과 기독교 신앙으로 형성된 문학적, 철학적인 통찰력을 시로 표현하고 싶은 강렬한 욕구가 불타올라 시를 쓰기 시작했다.

나의 주된 관심은 현대문명의 병폐를 진단하고 예술(가능성과 한계)과 신(God)(완전성)을 통해 그 해결책을 모색하는 것이었다. 이것은 다년간 교수 취업을 시도하는 가운데 부조리한 현실의 벽에 부딪히며, 사회 전반적으로 왜곡된 가치관과 구조적인 불공정이 뿌리 깊이 만연해 있음을 절감했기 때문이었다.

20여 년 한국에서 시작(詩作) 생활을 하던 중, 금년 초 몇몇 미국 시 사이트에서 활동을 시작하며 미국에서 시집을 출간하기로 결심하게 되었다. 이 시집을 통해 병든 문명 속에서 힘겹게 살아가는 세계 여러 나라의 독자들이 위로와 치유의 처방전을 발견하기 바란다.

2018. 11. 1. 김완수

Profile of the poet, Wansoo Kim

* Ph. D. (English Literature) from the graduate school of Hanguk University of Foreign Studies

* I was a lecturer at Hanguk University of Foreign Studies and an adjunct professor at Incheon Junior College for about 20 years.

* I published 5 poetry books, one novel, and one essay book etc.: one poetry book, "Duel among a middle-aged fox, a wild dog and a deer" was a bestseller in 2012, one page in the book of 'Letters for Teenagers' was put in the textbooks of middle school (in 2011) and high school (in 2014) in South Korea, and three books ("Easy-to-read English Bible stories", Old Testament in 2017, New Testament in 2018 and "Teenagers, I Support your Dream") were bestsellers.

* Theses: Coleridge's Poetry and the Concept of Imagination(master's thesis in 1986), Auden's Poetry: Criticism on Civilization and the Concept of Art(doctoral thesis in 1992)

* Rookie award (poetry) at the magazine of Monthly Literature Space in South Korea.

* World Peace Literature Prize at the 5th World Congress of poets for Poetry Research and Recitation in New York in 2004.

Contents

Part 1

The Diseased World

A Spider

A spider

That dreams a rainbow-colored dream,

Spinning the threads of desire

In a corner under the dark eaves.

Though no insects appear today

Like they did not yesterday,

It gasps entangled

Among the nets

Spun by itself.

But even moaning sometimes,

It sings the song of hope

Spinning another thread.

거미

어두운 처마 밑 한구석에
욕망의 실타래 풀어놓고
무지갯빛 꿈꾸는
거미 한 마리

오늘도 어제처럼
조그만 벌레 한 마리
얼씬대지 않건만

스스로 푼
실타래에 얽혀
가쁜숨 몰아쉰다

수시로 신음을 토하면서도
또 다른 실을 뽑아내며
희망의 노래를 부른다

A Strange Bag

He is all smiles

Humming

With only the expectation he may possess

He knows he won't be filled up

But he always opens his mouth

Just like a man exhausted with hunger.

He is proud of his possession,

But when lost or deprived,

He doesn't fall asleep or falls ill.

Laughing or weeping

With the things like the wind

That'll stay for a short time,

He opens his mouth

Just like a man exhausted with hunger.

이상한 자루

가질 거라는 기대만으로도
콧노래를 부르며
싱글벙글거린다

차지 않을 걸 알면서도
언제나 허기진 놈처럼
입을 벌린다

가진 걸 뻐기기도 하지만
잃거나 빼앗기면
잠 못 자거나 병이 난다

잠시 머물
바람 같은 것에
웃고 울며
허기진 놈처럼
입을 벌린다

Tears of the Moon

A woman who has come

Stepping lightly on the darkness

In yellow skirt and coat,

And white socks.

Why does she look around

With her big eyeballs?

Is it because she wants to see her lover?

In the whirl of flashes

Sharp like the edge of a knife

On the streets of blazing lamps and neons,

She's shedding only tears

With eyes blind and heart torn

Shrinking and lingering.

달의 눈물

노란 치마저고리
하얀 버선발로
살포시 어둠 딛고
찾아온 여인

그 누구
그리운 님을 찾기에
커다란 눈망울로
두리번거리나

번쩍이는 가등과 네온의 거리
칼날처럼 날카로운
번뜩임의 소용돌이에

눈멀고 가슴 찢겨
움츠리고 서성대며
눈물만 흘리네

A Philippine Child Digging the Trash Mountain

When a child looking like a schoolchild
Wakes up in the morning,
He runs to the trash mountain
And digs out grains of hope
Training the lens of his two eyes
On shabby rubber shoes or pieces of metal

If he digs up leftover bread
Or even sour milk fortunately,
He hurriedly thrusts it
Into the entrance door of the hose of his life
That pulls like a powerful magnet,
Without the time to look at its birthday.

The trash mountain
Is the life school
Without teachers and books
And the job without pay

When he comes back to his mother
With some pieces of musty treasure
With all his body black after dusk,
The diseased mother
Hugs with tears
His life weight over hundreds or thousands of kilograms
Tottering addicted to the trash odor.

쓰레기 산의 필리핀 아이

초등학생 또래 아이가
아침에 눈을 뜨면
쓰레기 산으로 달려가
낡은 고무신이나 쇳조각에
두 눈의 렌즈를 맞추고
희망의 알갱이들을 캔다

운이 좋아
먹다 남은 빵조각이나
상한 우유라도 캐면
출생일을 살펴볼 겨를도 없이
강력한 자석처럼 끌어당기는
생명의 호스 출입문으로
허겁지겁 쑤셔 넣는다

쓰레기 산은
선생님과 책이 없는
인생 학교
임금 없는 직장이다

해가 저물어
새까만 온몸으로
쾨쾨한 보물 몇 조각 들고
엄마 품을 찾으면
병든 엄마는
쓰레기 향 중독으로 비틀대는
수백 수천 킬로그램 삶의 무게를
눈물로 얼싸안는다

Children of Talebans

Teenagers
That even the blood of all desires is dried
By a whip of scary hunger every day
Hang all the hope of their life in Talebans' hands
Hung on the bait of free bread and free study.

Talebans light
A fire of hostility
In the heart of innocent children
With the brutal video
That Westerners killed Muslims.

They also light a fire of proud martyrdom in the children's heart
That a suicide bombing to aim at Westerners
Is the glorious way
To receive the eternal Heaven as a gift.

The children
Load the technique to make a bomb jacket and to kill people
In their heart blazing with hostility and martyrdom
And hurl all their life.

Even this moment a lot of children
With bombs wrapped around all their body as a band of glory
At a single motion
Burn their bud bright with jewels of their dream
And fly away reduced to ashes.

탈레반 아이들

날마다 무서운 굶주림의 채찍으로
모든 의욕의 피마저 말라버린
십 대 아이들이
공짜 빵과 공짜 공부의 미끼에 걸려
탈레반의 손아귀에
삶의 희망 전부를 건다

탈레반은
서양인이 무슬림을 죽인
잔혹한 영상으로
순진한 아이들의 심장에
적개심의 불을 지핀다

서양인을 겨눈
자살폭탄은
영원한 천국을 선물 받는
영광의 길이라고
자랑스런 순교의 불을 지핀다

아이들은
사람 죽이는 기술
폭탄 만드는 기술을
적개심과 순교심이 타오르는
심장에 장전하고
인생 전부를 던진다

오늘도
수많은 아이들이
폭탄을 영광의 띠로 온몸에 휘감은 채
꿈의 보석이 영롱한 꽃망울을
단 한 번에 불사르며
재가 되어 날아간다

An African Baby

A bony baby
Sheds tears without sound
Drooping at her mother's breast
As he has no purse of instinct
To ring the alarm sound of a hungry feeling,
And a bony diseased mother
Sheds tears like bloody pus
Putting her baby to the dead breast.

AIDS day by day
Pulls a lot of parents
To grave,
And the dirt wind,
Playing rolling for a few days
with a baby crying alone
In the dim mud hut,
Pulls it to grave.

AIDS that has sneaked
Into the mother's breast,
Hanging the invisible rope
On the neck of a newborn baby
Hard to keep its balance,
Pulls the innocent eyes
To grave.

Contagious disease,
Wandering around the refuge camp,
Pulls the cute little hands
That shed anxious tears
Tired of hunger
To grave.

아프리카 아이

뼈만 남은 아이가
엄마 품에 늘어져
허기증의 경보음을 울릴
본능의 맥박도 뛰지 않아
소리 없이 눈물을 흘리고
뼈만 남은 병든 엄마는
죽은 젖을 물린 채
피고름처럼 눈물을 흘린다

에이즈는 나날이
수많은 부모를
무덤으로 끌고 가고
흙바람은
침침한 움막 속에
혼자서 울고 있는 아이와
며칠 뒹굴며 놀아주다
무덤으로 끌고 간다

엄마의 젖줄에
몰래 침투한 에이즈는
가누기도 힘든
갓난아이의 목에
보이지 않는 올가미를 씌워
해맑은 눈동자를
무덤으로 끌고 간다

전염병은
난민 캠프 주변을
어슬렁거리며
굶주림에 지쳐
애타게 울고 있는
고사리 손을
무덤으로 끌고 간다

Classroom of Elementary School in Iraq

Sparkling eyes,
Which sit gathering
In the classroom
That has few desks and chairs,
Plant seeds of hope
In their hearts.

They write the teacher's words
In their hearts
Without the blackboard,
Books, and notebooks.

The booming of missiles
That often comes into hearing
Shakes the seeds of their dream to the roots
Tearing the childlike innocence of their heart.

During breaktime
Or when school is over,
Children, playing with the abandoned weapons like toys,
Are mortally wounded
In the sprout of their bright and untainted soul,
Or the whole blueprint of their life
Flies away in pieces.

이라크 초등학교 교실

책상도 의자도
몇 개 없는 교실이나
운동장 모퉁이
땅바닥에 모여 앉아
초롱초롱한 눈동자들이
꿈의 씨를
가슴에 심는다

칠판도 책도
공책도 없이
선생님의 말씀을
가슴에 적는다

수시로 들려오는
미사일 포성은
아이들 심장의 동심을 찢어대며
꿈의 씨를 뿌리째 흔든다

쉬는 시간이나 수업이 끝나면
아이들은 버려진 무기를
장난감으로 놀다
해맑은 영혼의 싹에
치명상을 입거나
삶의 설계도 전체가
산산조각 날아간다

An Afghan Child

A father gives his hungry child
Opium instead of bread,
Child having a tummy ache
Opium instead of medicine,
Crying child
Opium instead of candy.

Today the father as usual
Goes to work handing a bright smile
After throwing opium for breakfast
To his 4-year-old child,
While the child who became a slave of opium
Are taken to dreamland.

The child
Whose body and soul are tied all day
By the invisible chains of opium—
In which dreamland is he traveling?

아프간 아이

아버지는 배고픈 아이에게
밥 대신 아편을
배가 아픈 아이에게
약 대신 아편을
우는 아이에게
사탕 대신 아편을 준다

아버지는 오늘도 평소처럼
네 살배기 아이에게
아편을 아침밥으로 던져주고서
환한 미소 건네며 일터로 나가고
아편의 노예가 된 아이는
꿈나라로 끌려간다

하루 종일
아편의 보이지 않는 쇠사슬에
몸과 영혼이 결박된 아이는
어떤 꿈나라에서 여행하고 있을까

Ggotjebis of North Korea

The moment
That a running train stops,
The bloodthirsty light sparkles
From the eyes of the children
That have lain on the ground

The moment
That several of cookies and candies
Fly toward the children out of the windows,
The children, abruptly changing into wolves
Throw their whole body at the cookies or the candies.

All the children tussle
Letting out horrible shrieks,
And a small straggler
Who didn't catch even a candy
Sobs covered all over with dirt.

When the eyes looking out of windows
Are filled with tears for a while,
The train measuring time
Flies away raising a cloud of dust
Like a biting wind.

The children
Lying on the ground again
become dead bodies only breathing
And the cloud of dust
Plays a dead body game
Coiling them.

북한의 꽃제비들

달리던 열차가
멈추는 순간
땅바닥에 누워있던
아이들의 눈에서
살기 어린 광채가 번뜩인다

앞다투어 달려드는
아이들을 향해
과자와 사탕 몇 개가
창밖으로 날자
아이들은 이리떼로 돌변하여
온몸을 던진다

모두 다 괴성을 질러대며
난투극을 벌이고
사탕 한 개도 못 잡은
조그만 패잔병은
흙투성이가 되어
흐느낀다

창밖을 바라보는 눈들이
잠시 눈물을 글썽일 때
시간을 재고 있던 기차는
흙먼지를 일으키며
칼바람처럼 날아간다

아이들은 또다시
땅바닥에 누워
숨만 할딱이는 시체가 되고
흙먼지는 그들을 휘감고
시체놀이를 한다

Hurricane of America

As the sky bomber,
Sallying into New York,
The heart of the world civilization,
Loses a blow of the storm bomb,

The face of an arrogant superpower
Turns so pale
That it shakes in its boots
After turning off the nuclear plant
And the electricity power station.

Nuclear bombs,
High-tech missiles,
And supersonic fighter planes
Only beg for their life
Wringing their hands

At a single blow,
Not only a gigantic tree is broken
Only to crumble children and cars,
But also mountains collapse,
Houses fly away,
And millions of people
Flee for refuge.

As the sky bomber,
As if it decided to do something,
comes carrying a group of dark rainclouds
And poured wildly a tropical storm bomb
Into all over the city,
New York,
Screaming with a siren,
Only begs wringing its hands.

미국의 허리케인

하늘 폭격기가
세계 문명의 심장
뉴욕에 출격하여
폭풍 탄을 한방 날리자

거만했던 초강대국의 얼굴은
새파랗게 질려
원전의 발전기를 끄고
전기 스위치를 통째로 내린 후
사지를 벌벌 떤다

핵폭탄도
최첨단 미사일도
초음속 전투기도
꼼짝달싹 못 한 채
제발 살려달라고
두 손 모아 빌기만 한다

단 한 번의 폭격으로
거목의 목이 부러져
아이들과 차량이 콩가루가 되고,
산이 쓰러지고
주택이 날아가며
수백만 명이
피난길을 떠난다

하늘 폭격기가
뭔가를 작심한 듯
검은 비구름 떼를 싣고 와
열대성 폭풍 탄을
도시 곳곳에 마구 쏟을 때,
뉴욕은 사이렌으로 비명을 질러대며
두 손 모아 빌기만 한다

Tears of Glacier

In the jungle of buildings

City dances in all seasons

Falling in a hot love

With air conditioners or cars

Day and night.

A woman who has kept her virginity long years

In clothes of virgin white with loft pattern

Sobs growing thin day by day

With the pain

That the disease of repressed stress bursts her heart

And tears her internal organs

Because of the hot dancing wind

That city blows with his whole body and soul

The man that doesn't even turn his eyes on

Why the woman sobs

And what kind of serious disease she suffers from

Still today day and night

Burns his body

In flames of money and pleasure

With his blood boiling over

Due to the dancing wind.

빙하의 눈물

도시는
빌딩의 밀림 속에서
밤낮 에어컨이나 자동차와
열애에 빠져
사계절 춤을 춘다

고고한 무늬 순백의 옷 차려입고
오랜 세월 처녀성을 지켜온 여인은
도시가 온몸과 영혼으로 뿜어대는
뜨거운 춤바람에
울화병으로 가슴이 터지고
오장육부가 찢어지는 통증으로
날로 야위며 흐느껴 운다

여인이 왜 우는지
무슨 중병에 걸렸는지
눈길조차 주지 않는 사내는
오늘도 밤낮 가리지 않고
돈과 쾌락의 불로
제 몸 활활 태우며
춤바람에 피가 끓어 넘친다

Bread and Bombs

On the one side of the earth,

A hungry mother sobs

Because she does't put a piece of bread

Into the mouth of her crying child

Due to hunger.

On the other side,

So many sacks of money

Are poured

To stamp out bombs or missiles.

While pieces of metal

Are poured like rolls of paper money

From the sky,

The starved people hit by pieces of metal

Fly away in pieces

Like broken bread crumbs.

Those who have sacks of money

Say they pour bombs

To give something to eat and peace,

But those who are dizzy

Because the guts are dried up,

Look at poured pieces of metal

Like pieces of bread

Hearing their speech as a strange foreign language.

빵과 폭탄

지구 한쪽에선
허기진 엄마가
허기로 울부짖는 아이에게
빵 한 쪽 물리지 못해
흐느끼고

다른 한쪽에선
폭탄이나 미사일을
찍어내기 위해
수많은 돈 자루를
쏟아붓는다

하늘로부터 쇳조각이
돈다발처럼 쏟아지는데
쇳조각에 맞은
굶주린 사람들은
부서진 빵가루처럼
산산이 날아간다

돈 자루를 가진 자들은
평화의 나라와
먹을 것을 주기 위해
폭탄을 퍼붓는다 하고
창자가 말라붙어 현기증이 나는 사람들은
그들의 말을 낯선 외국어로 들으며
쏟아지는 쇳조각을
빵 조각처럼 바라본다

Bread and Bombs

On the one side of the earth,

A hungry mother sobs

Because she does't put a piece of bread

Into the mouth of her crying child

Due to hunger.

On the other side,

So many sacks of money

Are poured

To stamp out bombs or missiles.

While pieces of metal

Are poured like rolls of paper money

From the sky,

The starved people hit by pieces of metal

Fly away in pieces

Like broken bread crumbs.

Those who have sacks of money

Say they pour bombs

To give something to eat and peace,

But those who are dizzy

Because the guts are dried up,

Look at poured pieces of metal

Like pieces of bread

Hearing their speech as a strange foreign language.

빵과 폭탄

지구 한쪽에선
허기진 엄마가
허기로 울부짖는 아이에게
빵 한 쪽 물리지 못해
흐느끼고

다른 한쪽에선
폭탄이나 미사일을
찍어내기 위해
수많은 돈 자루를
쏟아붓는다

하늘로부터 쇳조각이
돈다발처럼 쏟아지는데
쇳조각에 맞은
굶주린 사람들은
부서진 빵가루처럼
산산이 날아간다

돈 자루를 가진 자들은
평화의 나라와
먹을 것을 주기 위해
폭탄을 퍼붓는다 하고
창자가 말라붙어 현기증이 나는 사람들은
그들의 말을 낯선 외국어로 들으며
쏟아지는 쇳조각을
빵 조각처럼 바라본다

Part 2

Science and Art

2부 과학과 예술

Science

A monster
With a big head
And so many bright eyes,
But small cold heart.

Though you act big pretending to know everything
Always tapping on a calculator
And arranging numbers
Looking into a microscope or telescope,

Aren't you a hardheaded rube
That doesn't know or feel
What is love
That two souls meet to become one?

Why did you, nevertheless, fly to the kingdom of the moon
Flapping the wings like a strong eagle
Only to kill a milling rabbit
And also fly to the kingdoms of the stars
Only to interrupt the love between the Altair and the Vega?

How do you sense the spring water of inspiration
Flowing out of the deep valley of the artist's soul
And shed light on God's providence
That Jesus was born
By the Holy Spirit resting on Mary?

과학

머리는 크고
눈은 많고 밝으나
가슴은 작고 차가운
괴물이여

늘 계산기를 두드리고
현미경이나 망원경을 들여다보며
숫자들을 늘어놓고
모든 것을 다 아는 척 으스대지만

두 영혼이 만나 하나가 되는
사랑이 무엇인지
알지도 느끼지도 못하는
고지식한 풋내기가 아니더냐

그런데도 왜 힘센 독수리처럼 날개를 퍼덕이며
달나라로 날아가
방아 찍는 토끼를 죽여 버리고
별나라로 날아가
견우와 직녀의 사랑을 가로막느냐

네가 어찌 예술가의 영혼 깊은 골짜기에서
흘러나오는 영감의 샘물을 감지하며
마리아에게 성령이 머물러
예수가 태어난
신의 섭리를 밝히겠느냐

Computer

To my son
Who sits face to face
At every opportunity,
A great lover
Who burns his two eyes and heart.

Even when he is tired of studying
Or he is gloomy
Or angry,

When he sends only the glitter of his eyes,
In a moment
It takes him to the land of fantasy
Filling his faded soul
With fresh vitality.

It pulls even his step,
Which hesitates to approach it
Afraid of his mother's nagging,
Like a power magnet
With a miracle drug of mysterious love.

But if one of its parts
Gets perverse,
A deceptive superman
That all comes to an end in a moment.

컴퓨터

틈만 나면
마주 앉는 아들에게
게임도 보여주고 노래도 들려주며
그의 두 눈과 심장을 불태우는
사랑꾼

공부가 싫증나거나
우울하거나
화날 때도

아들이 눈빛만 보내면
한순간에
시들은 영혼에
신선한 활력을 가득 채우며
환상의 나라로 데려간다

엄마의 잔소리가 무서워
다가서길 망설이는 발걸음도
사랑의 신비한 묘약으로
강력한 자석처럼 끌어당긴다

하지만 부속품 하나가
심술을 부리면
한순간에 모든 게 끝장나는
사기꾼 슈퍼맨

Spell (1)

She falls under a spell
At eight O'clock every night.

She, throwing aside her work,
Sticks at TV
Attracted by the magnet of a spell
Like a person
That the function all over the body is suspended.

Her soul,
Tuning in those of actors and actresses on TV,
Cries and laughs
like a person in another world.

On the moment,
The watch of worry and anxiety stops
And she can't hear
What children and husband say.

After a while,
When the soap opera has finished,
Her overflowing liveliness
Disappears somewhere
As if she were a person broken under the spell
And the watch of worry and anxiety
Works again.

She, however,
Already misses
Eight o'clock the next night.

마법 1

매일 밤 8시만 되면
그녀는 마법에 걸린다

하던 일을 팽개치고
마법의 자석에 이끌려
온몸의 기능이
정지된 사람처럼
TV 앞에 달라붙는다

그녀의 영혼은
배우들과 주파수를 맞추고
딴 세계 사람처럼
울고 웃는다

그 순간
걱정과 불안의 시계는 멈추고
아이와 남편의 말도
들리지 않는다

잠시 후
극이 끝나면
마법이 풀린 사람처럼
넘치는 생기는
어디론가 사라지고
걱정과 불안의 시계가
다시 작동한다

그래도 그녀는
다음 날 밤 8시를
벌써 그리워한다

Chamber Music Performance

High and low harmonies

Rush on the whole body

Becoming flexuous waves.

They raise the whirlpool of passion

In the heart drooping feebly

Pouncing as a mountain at one time

Or get back and pick up

The traces of memory erased long before

Permeating as ripples in small veins.

The fragments of memory

Make the whole body overflow with the river of yearning

Flowing hard in every vein

Turned into the current of joy or sorrow

According to the ripples of waves crashed.

실내악 연주

높고 낮은 화음이
굽이치는 파도가 되어
온몸에 밀려온다

한꺼번에 산더미로 덮쳐
힘없이 쳐진 심장에
격정의 소용돌이를 일으키는가 하면
잔물결로 실핏줄에 스며들어
지워진 지 오래된 기억의 흔적들을
되찾아 건져낸다

기억의 파편들은
부딪치는 물결의 파문에 따라
기쁨이나 슬픔의 물살이 되어
핏줄마다 여울져 흐르며
온몸을 그리움의 강으로 넘실대게 한다

Spell (2)

To the man
Who came back home
After finishing his hard work,
A song washes away his tiredness
Caressing his whole body
Like his lover's hands.

The melody and harmony
Flowing softly
Heals, in a moment,
The scar of his heart
That has been torn all day
And has the meaning of life
Chewed over.

The melody that spews like a fountain
Flies away like feathers
Even the shocking of wars or awful accidents
As well as anger and sorrow
That have been heaped long.

The spell of the song, however,
Isn't found even in its small traces
The next morning
And the dregs of anger and sorrow
Wriggle again like the devil
In the deep place of the heart.

마법 (2)

힘든 일을 마치고
귀가한 그에게
한 줄기 노래는
연인의 손길처럼
온몸을 애무하며
피로를 씻어준다

부드럽게 흐르는
선율과 화음은
하루 종일 찢어진
마음의 상처를
한순간에 치료하고
삶의 의미를
되새기게 한다

분수처럼 뿜어져 나오는 가락은
오랫동안 쌓였던
분노와 슬픔,
TV에서 흘러나오는
무서운 사건의 충격마저
깃털처럼 가볍게 날려버린다

하지만 노래의 마력은
다음 날 아침이 되자
작은 흔적조차 찾을 수 없고
분노와 슬픔의 앙금은
가슴 깊은 곳에서
악령처럼 다시 꿈틀댄다

House of a Poem

I'll build a house of a poem
Because it doesn't hand a piece of bread or a penny
But it can be a spring water of joy or comfort welling up
That a piece of bread or a penny cannot give.

I'll build a house of a poem
Because it doesn't make weapons to be able to win a war
But it can transfuse the blood of wisdom or courage flowing
To be able to prevent or win a war.

I'll build a house of a poem
Because it doesn't have a tyrant's knife
But it can be a teacher
To tame a tyrant's tongue.

I'll build a house of a poem
Because it doesn't have a clever scheme
To prevent time from carving wrinkles on my sweetheart's forehead
But it can be a book to keep forever
Her smiling face.

I'll build a house of a poem
Because it isn't a miracle medicine
To make the dead alive
But it can be a wonder medicine
To make the dying alive.

I'll build a house of a poem
Even tearing all the flesh of my soul to pieces
Because it doesn't prevent all the things of life
From going into the tomb
But it can be a work of art to make alive forever
Brilliant moments of disappearing things.

시의 집

시의 집은
밥 한 그릇이나 돈 한 푼 건네지 못하지만
밥이나 돈으로 줄 수 없는
기쁨이나 위로가 솟는 샘물이 될 수 있으니
시의 집을 지으리

시의 집은
전쟁을 이길 수 있는 무기는 만들지 못하지만
전쟁을 막거나 이길 수 있는
지혜나 용기가 흐르는 피를 수혈해줄 수 있으니
시의 집을 지으리

시의 집은
폭군의 칼은 없지만
폭군의 혀를 길들이는
스승이 될 수 있으니
시의 집을 지으리

시의 집은
시간이 연인의 이마에
주름살 새기는 걸 막을 묘책은 없지만
연인의 미소 짓는 눈동자를
영원히 간직하는 책이 될 수 있으니
시의 집을 지으리

시의 집은
죽은 자를 살리는
영약(靈藥)은 아니지만
죽을 자를 살리는
묘약이 될 수 있으니
시의 집을 지으리

시의 집은
인생사 모든 것이
무덤으로 들어가는 걸 막지는 못하지만
사라지는 것들의 빛나는 순간들을
영원히 살게 하는 예술품이 될 수 있으니
시의 집을 지으리
영혼의 모든 살을 갈기갈기 찢어서라도

Novel, "Our Twisted Hero"

The story of innocent children
Happening in the classroom
Makes us smile bitterly the sly political world
And becomes a cane to scold the twisted human nature,

So that it puts the laughing wind
Into the hard and exhausted heart,
Makes the heart of arrogant person
shed the tears of self-reflection,
And gives the heart of thoughtless person
Ripe experience and wisdom,

And it makes the flame of justice
Blaze up in the person blinded by self-interests
And becomes the medicine to revive conscience
In the heart of the decaying society.

But a novel
Is only a guide
To lead the way to truth
By the tongue of lie
That looks like truth,
And the novel can't be
A panacea suitable for different diseases
Or the Savior
To save the society of pain and despair.

It never chooses for itself
To console
Or to heal anyone,
But the temperature of its effect
Cannot but be different
According to the opponent to choose itself.

소설, "우리들의 일그러진 영웅"

교실에서 벌어지는
순진한 아이들의 이야기가
교활한 정치판을 쓴웃음 짓게 하고
뒤틀린 인간성을 나무라는 회초리가 되어

힘들고 지친 가슴에
웃음의 바람도 넣어주고
거만한 자의 가슴에
반성의 눈물도 흘리게 하며
철없는 자의 가슴에
풍부한 경험과 지혜를 주기도 하고

사리사욕에 눈먼 자에게
정의의 불길을
타오르게 하고
썩어가는 사회의 가슴에
양심을 되살리는 약이 되기도 하지만

소설은
진실처럼 보이는
거짓의 혀로
진리의 길을 인도하는
안내자일 뿐
서로 다른 질병에 맞는
만병통치약이 되거나
고통과 절망의 사회를 구원하는
구세주가 될 수도 없다

결코
스스로 선택하여
누군가를 위로하거나
치료하지 못하고
자신을 택하는 상대에 따라
효력의 온도도 다를 수밖에 없다

Looking at the picture, 'The Wild River'
By J.E.H. MacDonald
—at an art museum in Canada—

The snow-white
Rough river
Runs like a train
Into the middle
Of the deep red wild forest.

A picture like a poem
Spreads
Its own world
And catches the thoughts
Of the beholder.

It waits quietly
For the beholder
To spread the wings of imagination,
And try to guess
Or connect
This or that.

And the music
Flowing in the art museum
Doesn't hesitate
In the brain
Even for a moment
But surges into the heart
Enough to whirl the whole body.

J.E.H. 맥도날드의 그림
'거친 강'을 보며
—캐나다의 미술박물관에서—

희디흰
거친 강이
붉디붉은 거친 숲
한가운데로
열차처럼 달린다

시(詩)처럼 그림은
자신만의 세계를
펼쳐놓고
보는 이의
생각을 붙든다

보는 이가
상상의 날개를 펴고
이것저것
맞춰보거나
연결해 보라고
조용히 기다린다

그러나 박물관에서
흐르는 음악은
한순간도
머리에서
머뭇거리지 않고
가슴으로 밀려들어
온몸을 휘돈다

Part 3

Civilization and God

3부 문명과 하나님

Roars of Thunder

Rolling bang!
Those who have heartburn every day
To build a higher tower than that of others
Looking at just the earth.

Listen to roars of thunder
Before all the sands of life disappear
Crying because it's hard to erect a tower,
Crying looking at higher towers of others,
And crying because your erected tower has toppled down.

Rolling bang!
Don't follow only the law of the earth
That the flowers, which others look up to, bloom
When you heap more than others
Casting the dice on erecting a tower,
Because for me your tower or ones of others are alike,

But learn the law of the sky
That the flower garden, where all dance, is shaped
Because when beams of sunlight comes down
Sprouts of lives come out,
When the rain comes down
Leaves come out and flowers bloom,
When fruits fall down and die
More lives are born
And more flowers and fruits overflows.

천둥의 고함

우르릉 쾅
높은 탑을 세우려
날마다 가슴앓이하는 자들아

탑을 쌓기
힘들어 울고
높다란 남의 탑
쳐다보며 울고
쌓은 탑이 무너져 울다
인생의 모래알이
다 사라지기 전에
천둥의 고함을 들어라

우르릉 쾅
탑 쌓기에 모든 걸 걸고
남보다 많이 쌓아야
남들이 쳐다보는 꽃이 피는
땅의 법만 따르지 말고

햇살이 내려야
생명의 싹이 돋아나고
비가 내려야
잎이 나고 꽃이 피며
열매가 떨어져 죽어야
더 많은 생명을 낳고
더 많은 꽃과 열매가 넘쳐
모두가 춤추는
꽃동산이 되는
하늘의 법을 배워라

Christmas Eve

Here and there in front of the shopping area,
False Santas
Shake their handbell to open wallets,

Into the red mouth of a motel
That the electric sign with 'Merry Christmas' glitters,
Staggering young boys and girls are sucked,

At the corner of a subway station a Salvationist shakes a handbell,
The red frozen hands of a crouching homeless person
Are trembling due to the glares of the crowd,

In public houses, drunken people
Beat on the table with their chopsticks to carols
Chewing Jesus as a side dish,

In the nightclubs on the back streets,
Men and women intoxicated by light and music
Are burning their whole body and soul as a living sacrifice to Bacchus,

But in the sky, the tears of Jesus, snowing in large flakes
Pat all the people regardless of the homeless, the drunken, age or sex
Like mothers' hands.

성탄 전야

상가 앞 여기저기에서는
가짜 산타들이
지갑을 열기 위해 방울 종을 흔들고

'메리 크리스마스' 전광판이 번쩍이는
모텔의 붉은 입으로는
휘청대는 젊은 남녀들이 빨려 들어가고

구세군이 종을 흔드는 지하철역 모퉁이에는
웅크린 노숙자의 빨갛게 언 손이
군중의 눈초리에 떨고 있고

주점에서는 취객들이
예수를 안주로 씹어대며
캐럴에 맞춰 젓가락 장단을 두드리고

뒷골목 나이트클럽에서는
빛과 음악에 취한 남녀들이
주(酒)님께 온몸과 영혼을 산 제물로 불태우는데

하늘에서는 예수의 눈물이 함박눈으로 쏟아지며
노숙자, 취객, 남녀노소 가리지 않고
어머니의 손길처럼 어루만진다

A Compass

Please grab tightly
Legs shaking from side to side
Like those of a toddler.

If you hold one leg from the inside
And adjust its balance,
I'm likely to draw larger and farther
The traces of your heart
For you to leave to me.

If you loosen your clutching hands
Turning your eyes even for a moment
Or if you don't stand keeping your balance,
I'll drop or flop down at once.

Though I have often shaken off your hands
In the years when I wanted to wander at will,
I'm moved to tears now
Even feeling only your touch.

To be one with you eternally
Leaning as much as you lean
And erecting as much as you erect
Than to draw lots of big and nice pictures
Is my biggest dream.

컴퍼스

걸음마 배우는 아이처럼
좌우로 흔들대는 다리를
꼭 잡아주세요

그대가 안에서 한쪽 다리를 붙들고
균형을 맞춰준다면
그대가 나에게 남기는
마음의 흔적들을
더 크게 더 멀리 그릴 것 같아요

그대가 잠시라도 눈길을 돌리고
잡은 손을 느슨하게 풀거나
중심을 잡고 서지 않으면
그 순간 넘어지거나 주저앉을 거에요

제멋대로 나돌고 싶던 시절엔
그대의 손길을 뿌리친 적도 많지만
이제는 감촉만 느껴도
감격의 눈물이 흐른답니다

크고 멋진 수많은 그림을
그리기보다도
그대가 기우는 만큼 기울고
그대가 세우는 만큼 세워
그대와 영원히 하나인 것이
가장 큰 꿈입니다

Eyess

When I didn't know him,
The eyes of my heart were always
Toward the top of high stairs

And the eye lens brilliant with dreams
Focused on where the eyebeam of envy
And the applause of praise are.

At the beginning when I met him,
The eyes of my heart full of tears, moved deeply,
Overflowed with the song of thanks instead of shame
Covered with the deep color of his love
Even looking into all kinds of secret embarrassing parts in the heart
Attracted by his textbook on life.

At the moment when I go holding his living promise
And the guide he sent
Looking at him for decades,
Focusing on
His heart toward me,

The eyes of my heart
Adjust the angle of my tongue, arms and legs to 'it',
Often reading this clear phrase in his thought pocket:
'You are my family and heir.
Get the inheritance of my kingdom much
Due to the souls you bear and rear.'

시선(視線)

그분을 몰랐을 때
마음의 눈동자는 늘
높다란 계단 위로 향해 있었고

꿈으로 영롱한 수정체는
부러움의 눈빛과
찬사의 박수가 있는 곳에
초점을 맞추었다

그분을 만난 처음
감격으로 글썽이는 마음의 눈동자는
그의 인생 교본에 이끌려
마음속 은밀한 온갖 치부를 보면서도
그의 사랑의 진한 빛깔에 뒤덮여
수치심 대신 감사의 노래가 넘쳐났다

그분을 바라보며
그의 살아 있는 약속과 그가 보낸 길잡이를 붙들고
동행하는 지금
나를 향한 그의 마음에 초점을 맞추고

'너는 내 가족, 상속자
네가 낳고 기르는 영혼들로
내 나라 유산을 많이 받아라'
또렷한 글귀를 그의 생각 주머니 속에서
수시로 읽으며 혀와 팔다리의 각도를 조절한다

A Full Moon

The world where darkness gets deeper.
Though I look at him
Hoping to become the small mirror
To reflect his heart,

The mirror of my heart
Tends to be dim so easily
As I can't often see him
Or hear even any sense of him.

But you, a full moon,
Are shining the dark world every hole and corner
Smiling all over your face
Though the sun is not seen at all.
Moon, moon,
Whether you see the sun or not,
Are you conveying its heart to the core
Keeping up the bright mirror on your heart?

Do you know why I can't reflect the heart of him,
The father of all the lights
In the bright and untainted mirror
Even seeing the sun every day
And sensing its heart all over my body?

보름달

어둠이 짙어가는 세상
그의 마음을 비추는
작은 거울이 되고파
그를 바라보지만

수시로 보이지 않거나
기척조차 들리지 않아
마음의 거울이
희미해지기 일쑤인데

보름달, 너는
태양이 조금도 보이지 않건만
만면에 미소를 지으며
어두운 세상을 구석구석 비추고 있구나

오, 보름달
너는 태양이 보이든 말든
마음에 환한 거울을 달고
태양의 마음을 속속들이 전하고 있는 거니?

태양을 날마다 보고
그것의 마음을 온몸으로 감지하면서도
모든 빛의 아버지, 그의 마음을
왜 나는 해맑은 거울로 비추지 못 하는지
너는 알고 있니?

Cohabitation

To have often had a secret meeting
Since before meeting my wife
Without anyone knowing,

To whisper a secret conversation day and night
Being at the deeper place of the heart
Than that of my wife,

To wrap patting with the pathetic hands
Sensing the pain and the injury of my heart
Even though I don't say,

To pray with tears until I come back
Without pouring blame or anger
Even though I commit misdeeds
Sometimes turning my face away and keeping away,

He who has never shown even the eyebeam of any price or demand,
Whom I have never seen or heard anywhere in this world,
And who raises the wind of a deep emotion
Even beyond the border of love

Is my benefactor, the same body as my life
That has come flying from the sky like a dove
And that I can't detach myself from even for a moment
Even if anyone points the finger of any blame at me.

동거

아내를 만나기 전부터
아무도 모르게
수시로 밀회하는

아내보다도
더 깊은 마음의 자리에 있고
밤낮을 가리지 않고 밀담을 속삭이는

말하지 않아도
마음의 통증과 상처를 감지하고
애처로운 손길로 어루만지며 감싸주는

때로는 외면하고 멀리하며
비행을 저질러도
원망이나 분노를 쏟지 않고
돌아올 때까지 눈물로 기도하는

언제나 대가나 요구의 눈빛마저 보이지 않는
이 세상 어디에서 보거나 듣지 못한
사랑의 경계선 너머까지
감동의 바람을 일으키는 그는

누구에게 어떤 손가락질을 당해도
한시도 떨어질 수 없는
하늘에서 비둘기처럼 날아온
내 은인, 내 생명의 동체(同體)

A Mysterious Musical Instrument

Even a word or a motion
Becomes a string,
Which forms ripples
Carrying ardent stories of numerous vibrations.

A string of abuse spit harshly
Tears a heart to pieces
Or a string of staring eyebeams
Boils up the blood of the whole body.

A stream of the hands and feet of a certain action
Becomes the penalty of the heaven
Beyond the prison life on this earth
Or Becomes an eternal crown
Beyond the applause of everybody.

Looking, sometimes with the eyes of my spirit,
at the ears of the heaven pricked up
Even toward the rough and untuned play
Of its immature child,

I beat my chest
Wishing to form the ripples of the light and spring water
To the dark and faded hearts
With a string full of the heaven heart
Pouring off my thoughts every day.

신비한 악기

어떤 말이나 동작도
현(絃)이 되어
수많은 진동의 절절한 사연을 싣고
파문을 일으킨다

거칠게 내뱉은 욕설의 현이
마음을 산산이 찢기도 하고
노려보는 눈빛의 현이
온몸의 피를 부글부글 끓게도 한다

어떤 손발의 현은
이 땅의 옥살이를 넘어
하늘의 형벌이 되거나
만인의 박수를 넘어
영원한 면류관이 되기도 한다

철없는 자식의
거칠고 어그러진 연주에
쫑긋 세운 하늘의 귀를
영(靈)의 눈으로 때때로 바라보며

날마다 내 생각을 쏟아버리고
가득 찬 하늘 마음의 현으로
어둡고 시들은 가슴에
빛과 생수의 파문을 일으키게 해달라고
가슴을 친다

An Adopted Son

Master, am I your adopted son, right?

Even though I often ruminate
It's written in the legal document,
Why do I live as the servant of fear and anxiety
Bound up in fetters of doubt
Not dancing with the wings of joy?

Master, why don't you say
'You're my adopted son, right.'?

The phrase that you gave me even the right of inheritance
After tearing all the books of my misbehaviors
Without getting any price
Sounds like the fib of a boaster
In this place stolen from under the nose of the security guard.

If I read those syllables
With the heart like the children's eye,
The master's answer is likely to be heard,
But false information flies into my eyes and ears every day
And is stirring my heart dark;
What should I do?

Master, please look down into this heart
That writhes catching hold of only you
Even in the middle of the muddy water
And say just a few words,
'My dear son'!

양자(養子)

주인님, 제가 양자 맞나요?

법적인 문서로 쓰여 있다는 구절을
수시로 되새김질하면서도
왜 환희의 날개로 춤추지 못하고
의심의 족쇄에 묶여
두려움과 불안의 종으로 사나요?

주인님, '양자 맞다'
단 한 번만 말씀해주시면 안 되나요?

아무런 대가도 받지 않고
잘못된 행실의 장부(帳簿)를
다 찢어버리고
상속권까지 주셨다는 구절이
눈뜨고 코 베이는 이곳에서는
허풍선이 뺑처럼 들리기까지 하니까요

어린이 눈동자 같은 마음으로
그 음절들을 읽으면
주인님 대답이 들릴 것만 같은데
날마다 거짓 정보가 눈과 귀로 날아들어
마음을 시커멓게 휘젓고 있으니
어찌하면 좋을까요

주인님, 흙탕물 가운데서도
당신만을 붙들고 몸부림치는
이 마음을 굽어보시고
'사랑하는 아들아'
한마디만 해주세요 제발!

In the Middle of a Typhoon

Whenever the waves like mountains beyond mountains
Try to swallow
The pitching and rolling boat
Screaming like crazy,

As the lamp in my head flickers,
The muscles and joints of the whole body come loose
And the heart gets squeezed.

When I cry out toward the sky
Pouring out worry and fear
Closing my eyes tight,
I see the person
Who sleeps on the bow of the boat.

While my eyes are resting
On his quiet smile for a moment,
A bright lamp in my head lights up like magic
And a new strength surges up.

In no time,
I become 'the eye of a typhoon'
That looks at the violent waves with a smile
Humming to his breath.

태풍 한가운데서

산 넘어 산 같은 파도가
요동치는 배를
미친 듯이 괴성을 지르며
삼키려 할 때마다

머릿속 등(燈)이 깜빡거리며
온몸의 근육과 관절이 풀리고
심장이 조여 온다

두 눈을 질끈 감고
염려와 두려움을 펑펑 쏟으며
하늘 향해 절규하자
뱃머리에서 주무시고 계신
그분이 보인다

잔잔한 그분의 미소에
잠시 눈길이 머무는 동안
마법처럼 머리에 밝은 불이 켜지고
새 힘이 솟는다

어느새
그분의 숨결 따라 콧노래를 흥얼대며
세찬 파도를 미소 짓고 바라보는
'태풍의 눈'이 된다

An Earthworm

A stranger rarely seen ordinarily
Throws up his groan twisting all the body
Onto the hill
Where cruel steps come and go.

A low voice
Sounds deep in my heart
To the person looking at him like a hideous thing:
'Father, please do what you want, not what I want.'

To become the fertile sap of trees and grasses
As the essence that has melt up all his life
So that he can offer fragrant flowers to the heaven,
He who has walked along only the roads in the ground
Where even nobody's eyebeam infiltrates

To transfuse life-giving water
To the time-limited fatal patients
Who flounder in the whirlpool of desires
Filling only their own stomach,

Is a living transfiguration
Of the person who became the essence of eternal life
Tearing the flesh of his whole body and shedding its blood
After climbing the hill of Calvary.

지렁이

평소에는 보기 드문 이방인이
잔인한 발길이 오가는
언덕 위로
온몸을 뒤틀며 신음을 토한다

역겨운 흉물처럼 바라보는 자에게
나지막한 음성이
가슴 깊이 울린다
'아버지, 내 원대로 마시고 아버지의 원대로 하소서'

향기로운 꽃을 하늘에 드릴 수 있도록
온 생을 다 녹인 진액으로
나무와 풀의 기름진 수액이 되고자
그 누구의 눈빛조차 스며들지 않는
땅속 길만을 걸어온 그는

제 배만 채우며
욕망의 소용돌이에서 허우적대는
시한부 불치 병자들에게
생명수를 수혈하고자

갈보리 언덕을 올라
온몸의 살을 찢고 피를 쏟아
영생(永生)의 진액이 된 자의
살아 있는 변신이다

Double Vision

'One hour before the volunteer lecture'
When its alarm sounds throbbing,
The flame burning to nothing
Holds the strong hand of light to reach out suddenly
And hurries to press the phone number for a call taxi.

The flame drops the copious hot tears of its plea
Grabbing only the hand of light
While the buildings and cars out of the window
Are dancing doubly and dizzily.

When I open the door of the lecture room with my body nearly dead
After fighting objects desperately with my groping hands and feet,
The students blooming as twisted gypsophilas
Say good morning to me in a cheerful tune.

Though I have broken out in a cold sweat all over my body
To decode overlapped letters narrowing my eyes
Since the beginning of class with the tearful musical notes,

When I breathe a sigh putting the period of class,
The hand of light, enfolding the flame,
Whispers the syllables,"Great, great."
As a puff of the breeze.

Every street corner of life to fall into low spirits all over the body,
The temperature and the voice of the light hand
That enfolded my flame on that day
Are the vivid gospel to pour oil on the flame.

복시(複視)

'강의 봉사(奉仕) 한 시간 전'
경고음이 쿵쾅쿵쾅 울리자
사위어가던 불꽃은
어딘가에서 불쑥 내미는 강한 빛손을 붙들고
콜택시 전화번호를 서둘러 누른다

차창 밖의 건물들과 차들이
이중으로 현란하게 춤을 추어
불꽃은 빛손만 움켜쥐고
뜨거운 하소연을 주르르 떨군다

더듬대는 손과 발로 물체들과 사투를 벌인 끝에
초주검이 된 몸으로 강의실 문을 열자
일그러진 안개꽃으로 피어있는 수강생들이
경쾌한 음정으로 아침 인사를 건넨다

눈물 섞인 음표들로 수업을 시작하고
시선을 좁히며 겹쳐진 활자들을 해독하느라
온몸에 식은땀이 흘렀지만

수업의 마침표를 찍고 한숨을 내뿜자
빛손은 불꽃을 감싸 안고
'장하다, 장해' 음절들을
한 줄기 미풍으로 속삭인다

온몸에 맥이 풀리는 삶의 길목마다
그 날 안아주던
빛손의 체온과 음성은
불꽃에 기름을 붓는 생생한 복음이다

Part 4

South Korea

4부 한국

Haba Haba

Even when ordering food
Or taking a taxi,
Haba haba!

Those who have moved their tongue lightly
Saying that the blood of Korea
Boils and cools too fast
Cry "I like it because it's fast.
Korea best!"
As the Internet fever
Sweeps over the whole world.

The blood of Korea
That has bloomed
A source of mockery into that of pride
Is running like a wild horse
Toward another goal
Tirelessly,
And is shining
As the best weapon
That no one is hard to catch up with.

빨리빨리

음식을 주문하거나
택시를 탈 때도
빨리빨리

코리안의 피는
포르르 끓고 포르르 식는다고
혓바닥을 가볍게 놀려대던 자들이
인터넷 열풍이
온 세상을 휩쓸자
빨라서 좋다
코리아 베스트를 외친다

조롱거리를
자랑거리로 꽃 피운
코리아의 피는
지칠 줄 모르고
또 다른 고지를 향해
야생마처럼 달리며
그 누구도 따라잡기 힘든
최고의 무기로
빛나고 있다

World Cup Semifinals

Every night
The entire region of the Korean Peninsula
Became the sea of the Red Devils
And its wild waves swayed
According to every move of the players.

Every house
Stayed up all night
With shouts
And cars
Spent all night
With the festival of horns.

On the public squares
Strangers held hands like friends,
Strange boys and girls hugged like lovers,
And those who have hated
Shed the tears of reconciliation
Whenever a goal was scored.

The Red Devils' dream
Of "Dreams come true"
That had been seen very far away
Appeared before their eyes proudly
Every game
And hung a brilliant medal
Of the world semifinals
Around the neck of the whole nation,
Making the hot spring of blood gush
In the heart of all the people
Regardless of age or sex.

월드컵 4강

저녁마다
한반도 전역은
붉은 악마 바다가 되어
선수들 일거수일투족에
거센 파도가 일렁대었고
골이 터질 때면
우레 같은 축포가
한순간 전국에서
꽃피었다

집집마다
온밤을
함성으로 밝혔고
거리의 자동차들은
경적의 합주로
온밤을 수놓았다

광장에선
골이 터질 때마다
낯선 이들이
친구 되어 손잡았고
낯선 남녀들이
연인처럼 포옹했고
미워하던 이들이
화해의 눈물을 흘렸다

'꿈은 이루어진다'는
붉은 악마들의 꿈이
경기마다 눈앞에 펼쳐지며
세계 4강이라는 메달을
온 국민의 목에 걸어주고
남녀노소 모두의 가슴 속에
피의 온천이 용솟음치게 했다

Cry for the North Korea

The waves of civilization
Flow so fast
That we can fly
To China or Russia
Within half a day,

But in the North Korea land
That one blood flows,
What kind of river of grudge
Is so deep there
That even parents, brothers and sisters
Can't cross it
For over 60 long years?

In the North,
People go over the Tumen River
Casting away even their life
As they don't fill their empty stomach,
But in the South,
People pour a bundle of money into drugstores or clinics
As they don't lose the fat on their belly;
Is it OK to do so
Among parents, brothers and sisters with one blood?

It is said that last summer,
Even houses to lay their body down became like the sea water
Owing to the indiscriminate bombing of the sky;
Where do they sleep
And can they eat even any porridge?

Cry, the fat southern land.
Cry on your knees
Not making any excuses.
Don't you hear the groan
Of your starved parents, brothers and sisters?

북한을 위해 울어라

문명의 물결은
너무나 빨라
한나절이면
중국이나 러시아로
날아갈 수 있건만

한 핏줄이 흐르는 북한 땅은
무슨 원한의 강이
그리도 깊고 넓어
60여 년 긴 세월
부모 형제조차
건널 수가 없을까

북쪽에선
주린 배를 채우지 못해
두만강 물살에
목숨까지 내던지는데
남쪽에선
기름진 뱃살을 빼지 못해
약국이나 병원에 돈 보따리를 쏟아붓고 있으니
한 핏줄의 부모 형제간에
그래도 되는 걸까

지난여름엔 하늘의 무차별 폭격으로
몸을 누일 집마저
물바다가 되었다니
잠은 어디서 자며
죽이라도 먹는 걸까

배부른 남쪽 땅이여 울어라
아무런 변명도 하지 말고
무릎 꿇고 울어라
부모 형제 신음이
들리지도 않느냐

89

Cry for the South Korea

North Korea land,
Those whom you trampled with military boots
Shedding cannonballs
With your blood of hatred
More than 60 years ago:
Who were they to you?

Those living in the south
Whom you want to burn
Through the fire sea
As your blood of anger hasn't got cold
Although they send rice to you:
Who are they to you?

The bitter enemies
Whom you want to kill
With missiles and nuclear bombs
Gnashing your teeth:
What kind of mistake did they make to you?

Until when will your great leader be bragging
A strong and prosperous country,
And the earthly paradise,
While the people are bawling out
Due to their starvation
As days go by?

Cry, the northern land.
Cry beating your heart,
Not making any excuses.
Be young children
And cry your eyes out
Looking at the blue sky.

남한을 위해 울라

북한 땅이여
60여 년 전
증오의 피를 불태우며
포탄을 퍼붓고
군화로 짓밟은 자들은
그대의 누구인가

쌀을 보내줘도
분노의 피가 식지 않아
불바다로 태우고 싶은
남쪽에 사는 자들은
그대의 누구인가

미사일과 핵폭탄으로
죽이고 싶어 이를 가는
철천지원수들은
그대에게 무슨 잘못을 하였던가

날이 갈수록
백성들은
굶주림으로 흐느끼는데
그대의 위대한 지도자는 언제까지
강성대국과 지상낙원의 확성기를
틀어댈 것인가

북쪽 땅이여 울어라
아무런 변명도 하지 말고
가슴 치며 울어라
푸른 하늘을 바라보며
어린아이가 되어
펑펑 울어라

Korean Blast

Old Japanese women,
Crossing the East Sea(Japanese Sea) at a breath
To have the blood of youth transfused
Through their throbbing drama stars,
Burst cheers and tears
As teenage girls.

Young people with yellow hair
Jump up tearing their vocal cords
To the song whose meaning they don't know at all
Because K-pop gale blusters
In Europe and the American Continent
Where the hot blast of pop songs
Shook the young hearts of the Korean Peninsula
In my childhood.

The Korean hot blast
Crosses even the barbed-wire fence
Of the inter Korean border
And melts even the hostility like stone
Surrounded like Fort Knox
In the hearts of the soldiers taking a gun.

The Korean Peninsula now
Is not 'the land of the morning calm'
Or the land sobbing with grudges and sorrows any more
But the dreamland
With the living valcano of dramas and K-pops blazing
For the people of the world to wish to visit surely once.

한류 바람

나이든 일본 여인들이
가슴 뛰는 드라마 스타에게
청춘의 피를 수혈받으러
단숨에 동해를 건너와
10대 소녀가 되어
환호성과 눈물을 터뜨린다

어린 시절
팝송의 열풍으로
한반도의 젊은 가슴을 뒤흔들던
유럽과 아메리카 대륙에
케이 팝 광풍이 휘몰아쳐
노랑머리 젊은이들이
뜻도 모르는 노래에
성대를 찢으며 날뛴다

한류 열풍은
남북한 철조망까지 넘어가
총 든 병사들의 심장에
철옹성처럼 둘러친
적개심의 돌덩이마저 녹여버린다

이제 한반도는
더 이상 '고요한 아침의 나라'
한(恨)과 설움으로
흐느끼고 있는 땅이 아니라
세계인들이 꼭 한번 와보고 싶은
드라마와 케이 팝 활화산이 타오르는
꿈의 나라다

Dokdo Isle, Letter of Apology

Though you are a patriot who kept barehanded
The front line of his homeland for long years
Rooting the spirit like steel deeply
Even as the flesh pieces of your whole body are torn apart
And the bones of it are broken
By the knife blades of the waves wielded at any time
Holding hands with the wind and the rain flying from an island country

My love index about you
Was the figures
To chew your lyrics once or twice a year
like the gum to pass the time
And to pop the veins on my neck for a moment
Or click my tongue a few times
At the tongue that some Japanese sometimes wag like a black-faced bunting

The flowering plants to bloom genial smiles
Even Having the strings of their lives broken
By typhoon,
And the seagulls to throw up longing with a pathetic voice
Visiting in the middle of fighting for their life
As much as the wings fall out,

You are the models of the teachers
To show the high and blue fraternity
And the living scriptures that a vivid impression boils over
To me who can't bear to raise
My cheeky face.

I ask and ask patriotic martyrs
What I should do
To keep your long life
And light up your spirit like steel
Carving and carving every cell
The heart of the flowering plants and the seagulls.

    * Dokdo: a small isle between Korea and Japan:
     it has long belonged to Korea historically
     but the Japanese insist it should belong to them.

독도, 반성문

섬나라에서 날아오는 비바람과 손잡고
무시로 휘두르는 파도의 칼날에
온몸의 살점이 떨어져 나가고
뼈가 부서지면서도
강철 정신을 깊이 뿌리 내리며
긴 세월 조국의 최전선을
맨몸으로 막아낸 애국지사건만

나의 애정지수는
일 년에 한두 번 그대의 노랫말을
심심풀이 껌처럼 오물거리고
이따금 쪽발이들이 촉새처럼 놀려대는 주둥이에
잠시 핏대를 세우거나
혀를 두서너 번 차는
수치(數値)였다

태풍 속에
목숨줄 꺾이면서도
해맑은 미소를 피우는 풀꽃들아
날개가 빠지도록
바다와 사투를 벌이며 찾아가
애잔한 목청으로 그리움을 토하는 갈매기들아

두꺼운 얼굴을
차마 들 수 없는 나에게
너희는 높푸른 우애를 보여주는
스승의 표본이요
감동이 펄펄 끓는 살아있는 경전이다

풀꽃과 갈매기의 마음을
세포마다 새기고 또 새기며
그대의 만수무강을 위해
그대의 강철 정신을 빛내기 위해
무슨 일을 할 것인가
순국선열들에게 묻고 또 묻는다

Part 5

Politics and Various Lenses

5부 정치와 다양한 렌즈

Politics (1): Sorry, Politics

(Poems from politics (1) to politics (6) are the ones put in "Duel among a middle-aged fox, a wild dog and a deer", the bestseller poetry book written in Korean in South Korea in 2012.)

Whenever I thought of you,
Anger welled up
And I wanted to grab you by the collar
And beat you to be tired to death
Saying "boaster, swindler".

But even whenever I spoke ill of you knitting my brows,
I wanted to sing the song of happiness
Eating honey pouring out of your lips
With me just sitting or lying down

I who hoped to fly up like magic
Suddenly some day
Over the fence of hard and exhausting life
Was a foolish and greedy child.

정치 1 미안하다, 정치야

넌 생각하면
울화가 치밀어 올라
멱살부터 쥐고
허풍선이 사기꾼 하면서
녹초가 되도록 두들겨 패고 싶었다

눈살을 찌푸리고 욕을 하면서도 언제나
너의 입술에서 쏟아져 나오는 꿀을
그냥 앉아서 누워서 받아먹고
행복의 노래를 부르고 싶었다

어느 날 갑자기
너의 손을 잡고
힘들고 지친 삶의 울타리를
마법처럼 날아오르길 바란 내가
어리석은 욕심쟁이 아이였다

Politics (2): I'll kneel

From now on,

However hard and painful I am,

I won't draw the rainbow about you

Nor will I raise the voice of complaint and resentment.

From now on,

I won't turn my back nor will I avoid your eye

Like the couple in whom the dregs of disappointment and anger

Has been piled up for many years.

From now on,

Even though you do hateful or evil deeds,

I 'll become a mother with a sickly child,

Hug you shedding tears

Instead of a cane

And fold my hands falling to my knees

Worrying about your future.

정치 2 무릎 꿇을 게

이제는
아무리 힘들고 괴로워도
너에 대한 무지개를 그리거나
불평과 원망의 목청을 돋우지 않을 게

이제는
실망과 분노의 앙금이
오랜 세월 쌓이고 쌓인 부부처럼
등을 돌리고 눈길을 피하지 않을 게

이제는
네가 미운 짓을 하거나
몹쓸 짓을 저질러도
병약한 아이를 둔 엄마가 되어

회초리 대신
눈물을 흘리며 끌어안고
너의 앞날을 걱정하며
무릎 꿇고 두 손 모을 게

Politics (3): Please let him burn himself.

Heaven,

Please have pity on the person

Who said he would burn his blood and sweat

To be a servant of the people

But who burn the blood and the sweat of the people

In order to make his name shine.

If the embers to be a servant of the people

Remain even a little bit

In his heart,

Please let him burn his whole body

In order to light up the names of the people

With the use of the prayers of the people

Burning with the blood and the sweat

As kindling.

정치 3 자신을 불사르게 하소서

하늘이시어
백성의 종이 되기 위해
피와 땀을 태우겠다던 그가
자신의 이름을 빛내기 위해
백성의 피와 땀을
태우는 그를 불쌍히 여기소서

그의 가슴 속에
백성의 종이 되려는 불씨가
조금이라도 남아있다면
피땀으로 타오르는 백성의 기도를
불쏘시개로 사용하시어
백성의 이름을 빛내기 위해
온몸을 불사르게 하소서

Politics (4): Sound of silence

Whenever he opens his mouth,

He raises his vocal cords as much as possible

Saying he is smarter,

He has more possessions,

He has more experience than any others.

Heven,

Now let him listen to

The sound of silence

That the exhausted people whimper down in his heart

With his mouth closed firmly.

Please let him know soon

Many people are more eagerly waiting for

Those who listen opening their heart

To the sound of silence

Than those who cry out loudly.

정치 4 침묵의 소리

그가 입을 열면 언제나

누구보다 똑똑하고

가진 게 많고

경험이 많다고

목청을 한껏 높힙니다

하늘이시어

이제는 입을 굳게 다물고

주저앉고 쓰러진 자들이

가슴으로 울먹이는 침묵의 소리에

귀를 기울이게 하소서

다수의 사람들은

큰 소리 지르는 자보다

침묵의 소리

가슴 열고 듣는 자를

절절히 기다리고 있음을

그가 속히 알게 하소서

Politics (5): What can I say?

Even uprighting my head like a patriot

As I hurled all kinds of abuses

Often making my neck veiny

As I said if you changed

This country as well as this region would live well,

When the feast to change your face is held

Once every four years,

Even watching TV

Or taking a nap,

I threw not only a patriot's responsibility but also his right

Into a garbage can

As a waste paper or something like that.

I who just wanted you not only to be changed

but also to treat myself well

With my face turned away

Saying I hate to see even the face of you, a stupid sod:

What can I say?

With what face can I upright my head like a patriot?

정치 5 무슨 할 말이 있겠는가

네가 달라져야
이 고장 이 나라가 잘 산다고
수시로 목울대에 핏줄을 세우고
온갖 욕설을 퍼부으며
애국자의 콧대를 꼿꼿이 세우면서도

사 년에 한 번씩
너의 얼굴을 뒤바꿀 잔치가 열릴 때면
텔레비전을 보거나
낮잠을 자면서도
애국자의 권리도 책임도
휴지 나부랭이로
쓰레기통에 던져버렸다

꼴 보기 싫은 놈
낯짝도 보기 싫다고 외면한 채
네가 달라지기만
네가 잘해주기만 바랐던 자가
무슨 할 말이 있겠는가

무슨 낯짝으로 애국자의 콧대를 세우겠는가

Politics (6): Let's go to drive out the rotten river water

Those who look at the river

Folding their hands behind their back,

Even if they hurl abuses,

Spit,

And turn their back,

The rotten river water won't disappear by itself.

When all of us plunge into the rotten river water

And become a strong current

With the hearts where the blood of the holy anger

And the fervent prayer seethe,

The rotten river water will move back.

Let's go unfolding our hands behind our back

And plunge into the river.

If you and I don't do so,

The rotten river water won't disappear by itself.

정치 6 가자, 썩은 강물을 내몰러

뒷짐 지고
강물을 바라보는 자여

욕을 퍼붓고
침을 뱄고
등을 돌린다고
썩은 강물이 저절로 사라지진 않으리

우리 모두
거룩한 분노와
간절한 기도의 피가 펄펄 끓는 심장으로
강물에 뛰어들어
거센 물살이 될 때
썩은 강물은 물러나리

가자, 어서 뒷짐을 풀고
강물에 뛰어들자
너와 내가 뛰어들지 않으면
썩은 강물이 저절로 사라지진 않으리

Two dangerous children

One child who likes
The game of missiles and nuclear tests
And the other child who takes pride in
The game of aircraft careers and combat planes
Met at one place.

Those who have thrown murderous punches
Putting on the look of the devil
Whenever they open their mouth
Hand the flowers of a bright smile
Holding each other's hands like great friends.

Watching the two who show the pose
Like the great men supposed to get Nobel Prize,
The eyes in the whole world
Twinkle the colors of hope and doubt at the same time.

Will the unification festival happen,
Which applauses and cheers are so high all over the world,
In South and North Korea soon like a romantic drama?
Or will the crazy fear festival happen
Which lets out horrible shriek and blows up sparks
With missiles and combats planes losing their reason?

The eyes in the whole world
Raise the prayer letters for peace to the heaven day and night
Watching the mouths of the capricious children.

I also pray the braggart child with a big nose who likes flattery
Won't hurt his big nose
Looking down on the bright smile of the fatty child
Disguised as the innocent and humble eyes.

위험한 두 아이

미사일과 핵실험 게임을
좋아하는 아이와
항공모함과 전투기 게임을
자랑하는 아이가
한 자리에 만났다

입만 열면
악마의 표정을 지으며
살인적인 펀치를 날리던 자들이
다정한 친구처럼 손을 맞잡고
환한 미소 꽃을 건넨다

노벨상을 받을 위인들 같은
자세를 보여주는 그들을 보고
온 세상 눈동자들은
희망과 의심의 빛깔을 동시에 반짝인다

로맨틱 드라마처럼 조만간 남북한에
온 땅 구석까지 박수 소리와 환호성이 드높은
통일 축제가 벌어질까
아니면 미사일과 전투기가 이성을 잃은 채
괴성을 질러대고 불꽃을 터뜨리는
광란의 공포 축제가 벌어질까

온 세상 눈들은
변덕쟁이 아이들의 입을 주시하며
밤낮으로 평화의 기도문을 하늘에 올린다

아부를 좋아하는 허풍쟁이 코 큰 아이가
순진하고 겸허한 눈빛으로 위장한
뚱보 아이의 해맑은 미소를 얕보다가
큰 코 다치지 않기를 나 또한 빈다

To the Poem of a Flower

In front of darkness
That doesn't bloom a stem of a poem
Even though I burn my whole body
Staying up all night,

You are giving off
The mysterious scent
As the poem of a fresh flower
That petals are in full bloom.

In your white and clean flower flesh,
The myth of Venus is heard
And in your flower eyes like jewels,
The legend of Emerald Lake glitters.

Please don't open
Your reddish flower lips,
'Cause the whispers of love overflow
Even in the crack of the closed flower lips
And light a fire in the heart of darkness.

Darkness runs away
As you shine brilliantly,
But small embers
Left in the trembling heart
Are blooming
As a stem of a love poem.

한 송이 시(詩)에게

온밤을 지새워
온몸을 불살라도
한 줄기의 시
피우지 못하는 어둠 앞에

그대는 꽃잎이 활짝 핀
싱그러운 한 송이 시로
신비로운 향기를
내뿜고 있소

희맑은 꽃살에선
비너스의 신화가 들리고
보석 같은 꽃눈에선
에메랄드 호수의 전설이 반짝이오

발그레한 꽃술은
제발 열지 마오
다문 꽃술 틈으로도
사랑의 밀어가
넘쳐 나와
어둠의 가슴에 불을 붙이오

그대가 눈부셔
어둠은 달아나지만
떨리는 가슴에 남은
작은 불씨는
한 줄기 연시(戀詩)로
피어나고 있소

Life

Grass
Which lives eating dreams
And disappears like dreams.

Without eating dreams,
It'll be fallen leaves
Blooming only flowers of tears
Withering or getting sick.

But with eating dreams without stopping,
It'll bloom a flower
To touch the bitter hearts
With its fragrance made long
By tears and scars,
Even though shaken and soaked by the storms.

The sky often whispers
Patting it on the shoulder
No flowers bloom
without being shaken or soaked.

삶

꿈처럼 태어나
꿈을 먹고 살다가
꿈처럼 사라지는
풀이여

꿈이 없이는
시들거나 병들며
눈물 꽃만 피우다
낙엽 되지만

쉬지 않고 꿈을 먹으면
폭풍우에 흔들리고 젖는다 해도
눈물과 상처로
오랜 세월 빚은 향기로
쓰라린 가슴 어루만지는
꽃을 피우리

기우뚱대거나 젖지 않고
피는 꽃은 없다고
하늘이 종종
어깨를 토닥이며 속삭여준다

A Chair game

Chairs are 9
And people are 10.
One who doesn't occupy a chair
Is to die.

Next, chairs are 8
And the people are 9.
One of them again
Is to die.

The game never stops,
And the people, afraid that they may lose their life,
Shake their legs
With their faces got white
Even before it begins.

Though all of them run
Toward the chairs
At the same time as its beginning,
Surely one
Is to die.

Though all the family pray
With no sleep,
The owner of chairs not only picks up the one to die
With his icy hands
But also vigilantly tries extending his hands
Even to the remaining people.

No one enjoys the game,
But day by day,
it spreads out further and further
And corpses and wailings cover
All over the earth.

의자 놀이

의자는 아홉 개
사람은 열 명
의자를 차지 못하는 사람은
죽는 것이다

다음엔 의자는 여덟 개
사람은 아홉 명
누군가 또 한 사람
죽어야 한다

게임은 멈출 줄 모르고
사람들은 목숨을 잃을까
시작도 하기 전에
얼굴이 하얗게 질리고
다리가 후들후들 떨린다

시작과 동시에
모두 다 재빨리
의자로 달려가지만
반드시 한 사람은
죽을 운명

온 가족이 잠 못 자며
빌어보지만
의자 주인은 얼음 같은 손으로
죽을 사람을 골라내는 것 말고도
남아있는 사람들마저
호시탐탐 손길을 뻗쳐본다

즐기는 사람은 아무도 없는데
날이 갈수록
게임은 점점 번져나가고
시체와 통곡 소리가 온 땅을 덮는다

\<Review 1\> by Dustin Pickering (a poet, critic and publisher)

The increasingly complex world-society we live in today allows little room for reflection. Technology fuels growth and sophistication while the population increases exponentially. The old plagues are still with us: famine, disease, war, and poverty. These social ills overwhelm us and often make us feel powerless.

In Prescription of Civilization, Kim tackles these harsh truisms. He is willing to look at them both objectively and sympathetically. In the poem "Science" he writes:

Though you act big pretending to know everything

Always tapping on a calculator

And arranging numbers

Looking into a microscope or telescope,

Aren't you a hardheaded rube

That doesn't know or feel

what is love

That two souls meet to become one?

In these stanzas, Wansoo Kim divorces himself of modern conceptions out of frustration with their lack of human desire and spirit. We are often told science can eliminate the worst of human problems. In all truth, it is working hard to improve the human condition. This, however, does not distance us from its over-rationalizations and lack of humanism. The poet here introduces us to an often overlooked insight. The contemporary world is difficult precisely because the humanity we wish to save is lost in the very means we employ to save it.

Early verses in this collection serve as reminders of the worst of disasters humans have inflicted on their fellow humans. The poet's broad range of experience helps him identify with suffering all over the globe. As a South Korean, he is sorely hurt by the suffering in neighboring North Korea.

Kim further writes:

Even though I often ruminate

It's written in the legal document,

Why do I live as the servant of fear and anxiety

Bound up in fetters of doubt

Not dancing with the wings of joy?

There is a distinct sense reflected upon in this poem "An Adopted Son". The poem is a Christian plea to fellow Christians. An exclamation of joy in the resurrection of Jesus Christ is a cry of relief at the human condition. In an earlier poem, "Tears of the Moon", the moon is personified as a woman who has lost her lover. The ultimate symbolism is how distant we are from approaching Creation as a work of art to be appreciated. In neglecting to live in awe of Creation and instead see her as an instrument of our devices, we banish the Creator and disappoint Him. Civilization then is our downfall if we refuse to understand its ultimate purpose.

Kim reminds his readers that the sound and the fury of life is necessary for our redemption—our despair turns us into children seeking a Father; we become again as babes. This is the meaning of resurrection for us. In this startling realization, Wansoo Kim is in league with admirable poets and mystics like Rumi.

The Abrahamic faiths are powerful for the fact that they open the mind to spiritual dimensions and truths that the wise can perceive. In Proverbs 9:10, Solomon writes, "The fear of the Lord is the beginning of wisdom and the knowledge of the Holy One is understanding." Yet fear is not the act of being afraid. It is the sense of being alone in dread and anxiety, the existential condition. It is in realizing that your salvation depends on acknowledging you are a creation, a being wisely framed and entrusted with a task. Reverence and awe are rooted in fear. The sacred sense is developed by learning to approach objects of veneration with calm resolution. When an object, whether of contemplation or being, is properly understood it is given its faith because the faith within it is realized.

In "House of a Poem", the poet reflects on the meaning of art itself, especially the art of poetics:

I'll build a house of a poem

Even tearing all the flesh of my soul to pieces

Because it doesn't prevent all the things of life

From going into the tomb

But it can be a work of art to make alive forever

Brilliant moments of disappearing things.

Poetry is life and life is poetry. We cannot escape our mortality, but we can preserve the most uplifting of our sentiments and moments in history. Our struggles and dreams are kept within the glass of poetic sensibility like the objects of reverence previously mentioned. Poets can live in a state of awe, deep reflection, and mystery at once. John Keats called this state "negative capability". Kim astonishes the reader with his ability to be entranced in this state in works such as "Tears of the Moon". The poem is a cry for the lost humanity that becomes a victim in a long war against vulnerability and prayer. In a sense, the poem "House of a Poem" recognizes that civilization is humanity's Nature. We are creating a world of our own through work and self-domestication. Yet something must relieve us of our fears and hopelessness. We must re-lease tension from the bitter efforts of the day somehow. Kim gives us the reason for the arts—they relax us, reflect our deepest emotions, move the spirit, and keep us in touch with the reason we live. The arts are a prescription for civilization as well.

It seems as though Kim's prescription for civilization is recognizing the reality of life's purpose, of stepping away from the pragmatic capitalism that considers only use-value, distraction, entertainment, and profit. Did God condemn greed, gluttony, lust, and the like because these primal vices anchored us in materiality rather than the search for spiritual depth? As we remember the words of the Preacher in Ecclesiastes, "All is vanity!" it is safe to say that this truth is understood but ignored. The world doesn't seek God. The fundamental revelation in the Scriptures is that God alone is rest, shelter, and peace. Material comforts are short-lived and ephemeral. Too much obedience to the world and its will is a recipe for disaster—each person is created distinctly, given a purpose and pursuit of happiness, and faces a challenge to love fully. The enjoyment of the arts, the exercise of restraint and compassion, and struggling against the dark principalities are the true wellsprings of life.

Suffering is something we cannot eliminate entirely. We try to reduce it and often it takes us when we least expect it. Civilization is cause for a curse, but it makes individual lives more fulfilling and challenging. Christians believe that Jesus Christ suffers with them and they are not alone. This is the meaning of the Crucifixion. With Christ's resurrection, we are granted immortality. Through death and resurrection, Jesus saves our souls.

The prescription for civilization, then, is a holy devotion to Christian principles. The fact we need a prescription shows us what sort of malady causes our suffering. While other humans are not to be trusted, God Himself was willing to lay his own life down to testify to His mercy. Living within civilization is stress and life is a disappointment, but a reminder that Love is universal and we are all deserving of it is a positive message. Kim writes this collection not for moral instruction or harsh denunciation, but for the purpose of offering hope in a bleak world of continuous conflict and misery.

In the poems, we see a man who is raised from the death of his fears and desires into the proper understanding of living. Forgiveness is a release from debt. Christ's Passion was a forgiveness of all debts. His final moments on the Cross tell us that he wanted the redemption of sinners—even in their last moments. He knew human nature because he was human and divine. In his understanding, he too wrote a prescription for human suffering. The forgiveness of sins, unbridled compassion, pity for those unfortunate, and strong faith in God and His plan are Jesus' living legacies.

Kim realizes the need the world has for such a message and explores it in Prescription for Civilization creatively and fondly. His anger, sadness, fear, and doubt are all on display to remind us of our humanity. This is a task only a poet accepts.

서평 1 (Dustin Pickering의 review)

점점 더 복잡해지는 오늘날 세계사회는 숙고의 여유를 거의 허용하지 않는다. 인구가 기하급수적으로 증가해가는 반면에, 과학기술은 성장과 세련에만 주력하고 있다. 그럼에도 불구하고 기근, 질병, 전쟁, 가난과 같은 오래된 재앙들은 여전히 우리와 함께 존재한다. 이러한 사회적인 병폐들은 우리를 압도하며 종종 우리에게 무력감을 느끼게 한다.

〈문명의 처방전〉에서 김 시인은 이 냉혹하고 자명한 이치를 치열하게 파고든다. 그는 그것을 객관적이면서도 공감의 관점으로 기꺼이 바라본다. 〈과학〉이라는 시에서 다음과 같이 언급한다.

(상략)
늘 계산기를 두드리고
현미경이나 망원경을 들여다보며
숫자들을 늘어놓고
모든 것을 다 아는 척 으스대지만

두 영혼이 만나 하나가 되는
사랑이 무엇인지
알지도 느끼지도 못하는
고지식한 풋내기가 아니더냐
(하략)

— 〈과학〉 부분

124

위의 두 연(聯)에서 김 시인은 인간의 욕망과 정신의 결핍으로 인한 좌절감 속에서 현대적 관념들〔과학에 대한 통념들〕과 구별된 입장에 선다. 우리는 과학으로 최악의 인간 문제들을 없앨 수 있다는 말을 종종 듣는다. 진정, 과학은 인간 조건을 개선하려고 열심히 애쓰고 있다. 하지만, 지나친 합리화〔지나치게 이론적으로 설명함〕와 인도주의의 부족으로 인해, 우리를 과학의 문제점에서 벗어나게 해주지 못하고 있다. 이 점과 관련하여 시인은 보통 사람들은 흔히 간과하기 쉽지만, 시인만이 지닌 독특한 통찰력의 세계로 우리를 안내한다. 우리가 회복하기를 원하는 인간성이 그것을 회복하기 위해 우리가 이용하는 바로 그 수단 속에서 상실되기 때문에, 현대 세계는 곤경에 처해 있다고 보는 것이다.

이 시집에 수록된 앞부분의 시들은 인간들이 동료 인간들에게 가한 재난들 가운데 최악의 것을 상기시키는 역할을 한다. 시인의 폭넓은 경험은 그가 온 세계의 고통과 공감하는 과정을 수월하게 해준 것 같다. 남한 사람으로서 그는 이웃하는 북한의 고통 때문에 유독 마음 아파한다.

김 시인은 더 나아가 다음과 같이 쓴다.

(상략)

법적인 문서로 쓰여 있다는 구절을

수시로 되새김질하면서도

왜 환희의 날개로 춤추지 못하고

의심의 족쇄에 묶여

두려움과 불안의 종으로 사나요?

(하략)

　　　── 〈양자〉 부분

〈양자〉라는 시에서 주의 깊게 다루는 분명한 관념이 있다. 이 시는 동료 기독교인들에 대한 기독교인의 탄원이다. 예수 그리스도의 부활에서 기쁨의 절규는, 죽을 수밖에 없는 인간 조건에 대한 구원의 외침이다. 이 시보다 앞에 수록된 시, 〈달의 눈물〉에서, 달은 연인을 상실한 여인으로 의인화되어 있다. 〔노란 치마저고리/ 하얀 버선발로/ 살포시 어둠 딛고/ 찾아온 여인/그 누구/ 그리운 님을 찾기에/ 커다란 눈망울로/ 두리번거리나// 번쩍이는 가등과 네온의 거리/ 칼날처럼 날카로운/ 번뜩임의 소용돌이에// 눈멀고 가슴 찢겨/ 움츠리고 서성대며/ 눈물만 흘리네//〕 궁극적인 상징적 의미는 우리가 신의 창조물을 감사해야 할 예술 작품으로 접근하는 것으로부터 너무나 동떨어져 있다는 것이다. 신의 창조에 대한 외경심으로 사는 것을 등한히 하고 그 대신에 신의 창조물을 인간의 고안물 중의 한 가지 도구처럼 바라볼 때, 우리는 창조주를 추방하고 그를 실망케 하는 것이다. 그러므로 우리가 문명의 궁극적인 목적이해를 거부한다면, 문명이 우리의 파멸을 초래한다.

김 시인은 독자들에게 우리의 구원을 위해서 삶의 소란과 격정이 필요함을 상기시킨다. 즉 우리는 절망 때문에 하나님 아버지를 찾는 자녀들이 된다. 요컨대, 우리가 다시 아기들이 되는 것이다. 이것이 우리를 위한 부활의 의미이다. 이러한 놀라운 인식능력을 지닌 점에서, 김 시인은 칭찬할만한 시인들과 루미(Rumi) 같은 신비주의자들의 동류에 속한다.

아브라함 계통의 종교들은 현명한 사람들이 인지할 수 있는 영적인 차원과 진리에 마음을 열게 한다는 사실 때문에 영향력이 있다. 잠언 9장 10절에서, 솔로몬은 다음과 같이 기록한다. "여호와를 'fear' 하는 것이 지혜의 근본이요 거룩하신 자를 아는 것이 명철이니라." 그러나 'fear'는 공포가 아니다. 그것은 실존의 상태인, 두려움과 불안 속에 혼자 있다는 의식이다. 그것은 당신이, 지혜롭게 구상되고 어떤 임무가 부여된 존재인 신의 피조물임을 인정할 때 구원이 온다는 것을 깨달음에 있다. 경의와 외경은 'fear'에 뿌리박고 있다. 신성한 인식은, 차분하지만 결단력 있게 경의의 대상에 접근하는 방법을 배움으로써 개발된다. 명상에서든 실재에서든, 대상이 적절히 이해될 때, 그것에는 믿음이 부여되며, 그 이유는 그 내면에 있는 믿음이 깨달아지기 때문이다.

〈시의 집〉이라는 시에서, 시인은 예술 자체, 특히 시학이라는 예술의 의미를 숙고한다.

(상략)
시의 집은
인생사 모든 것이
무덤으로 들어가는 걸 막지는 못하지만
사라지는 것들의 빛나는 순간들을
영원히 살게 하는 예술품이 될 수 있으니
시의 집을 지으리
영혼의 모든 살을 갈기갈기 찢어서라도

— 〈시의 집〉 부분

시는 삶이고 삶은 시다. 우리는 죽을 수밖에 없는 운명을 회피할 수는 없지만, 우리의 가장 고양된 정서와 역사적 순간들을 보존할 수 있다. 우리의 투쟁들과 꿈들은 이전에 언급된 경의의 대상들처럼 시적인 감수성의 유리 진열장 내부에 보관된다. 시인들은 외경과, 깊은 숙고와 동시에 신비의 상태에서

살 수 있다. 존 키츠는 이러한 상태를 "네거티브 케이퍼빌러티"(negative capability)라고 불렀다. 김 시인은 〈달의 눈물〉과 같은 작품들에서 이러한 상태에서 황홀경에 빠지는 능력으로 독자를 놀라게 한다. 그 시는 상처받기 쉬운 마음과 기도와의 오랜 투쟁에서 희생물이 되는, 상실된 인간성에 대한 외침이다. 어떤 의미에서, 〈시의 집〉이라는 시는 문명이 인간성의 본성이라고 인식한다. 우리는 일과 '자기 길들이기' 〔인간이 스스로 동물적 본능을 억제하고 사회에 맞추어 가는 과정〕를 통해 우리 자신의 세계를 만들어 가고 있다. 그러나 무언가는 우리에게서 우리의 두려움과 절망을 완화해주어야만 한다. 우리는 어떻게든 날마다 그날의 혹독한 노력에서 유발되는 긴장을 누그러뜨려야 한다. 김 시인은 우리에게 예술의 이유를 제시해준다. 즉, 예술은 우리에게서 긴장을 풀어주고, 우리의 가장 깊은 정서를 반영하고, 정신을 움직이고, 우리의 존재 이유를 일깨워준다. 따라서 예술 또한 문명의 처방전이다.

김 시인의 문명의 처방전은 사용가치, 기분전환, 오락과 이익만을 고려하는 실용적인 자본주의로부터 거리감을 두고, 삶의 목적의 실체를 인식하고 있는 것처럼 보인다. 하나님은, 이러한 〔탐욕과 같은〕 원초적인 악덕들이 정신적 깊이의 추구보다는 오히려 물질성에 우리를 고정시키기 때문에, 탐욕, 대식, 색욕 등을 비난했을까? 우리가 "모든 것은 헛되다!"는 전도서 설교자의 말을 기억하므로, 이러한 진리가 이해는 되지만 무시되고 있다고 말하는 것이 안전하다. 세상은 하나님을 추구하지 않는다. 성경에 있는 근본적인 계시는 하나님만이 안식이고 피난처고 평안이라는 것이다. 물질적인 위안은 단명하고 덧없다. 세상과 세상의 뜻에 지나치게 복종하는 것은 재난의 처방전이다. 각 사람은 서로 다르게 창조되었고, 행복의 목적과 추구가 부여되었고, 마음껏 사랑하고자 하는 도전에 직면해 있기 때문이다. 예술의 향유, 절제와 동정의 실행, 어두운 세력들에 대항하는 투쟁은 삶의 진정한 원천이다.

고통은 우리가 완전히 제거할 수 없는 대상이다. 우리는 고통을 줄이려고 애를 쓰지만, 흔히 거의 기대하지 않을 때 고통이 우리를 덮친다. 문명은 저주의 원인이지만, 개인의 삶을 더 성취 지향적이고 도전적으로 만든다. 기독교인들은 예수 그리스도가 자신들과 함께 고통을 겪으므로 그들이 혼자가 아니라고 믿는다. 이것이 예수가 십자가에 죽은 의미이다. 그리스도의 부활과 함께 인간에게 영생이 주어졌다. 죽음과 부활을 통해서, 예수는 인간의 영혼을 구원한다.

그러므로 문명의 처방전이라는 시집은 기독교적 원리를 따르는 거룩한 헌신이다. 우리가 처방전이 필요하다는 사실은 어떤 종류의 병폐가 우리의 고통의 원인이 됨을 우리에게 보여주는 것이다. 타인들은 신뢰할 수 없는 대상이지만, 하나님 그 자신은 그의 자비를 증거하기 위해 자신의 생명을 기꺼이 희생하고자 했다. 문명 안에서 사는 것은 스트레스이고 삶은 실망스러운 것이지만, 하나님의 사랑이 보편적이고 우리 모두 그 사랑을 받을 만한 가치가 있음을 상기시켜주는 것은 긍정적인 메시지이다. 김 시인은 도덕적인 교훈이나 냉혹한 비난을 위해서가 아니라, 지속적인 갈등과 비참한 상황이 전개되는 황량한 세상에 희망을 제공하려는 목적으로 이 시집을 쓴 것이다.

시편들 속에서, 우리는 자신의 두려움과 욕망의 죽음으로부터 부활하여 삶에 대해 적절히 이해한 한 사람을 본다. 용서는 빚을 면제해주는 것이다. 그리스도의 수난은 모든 빚의 용서였다. 십자가 위에서 그의 최후의 순간들은 그가 죄인들의 구원, 심지어는 죄인들의 마지막 순간에 있어서조차도 구원을 원했음을 우리에게 말해준다. 그는 인간인 동시에 신이었기 때문에 인간성을 알았다. 그러한 이해 속에서, 그는 또한 인간 고통의 처방전을 쓴 것이다. 죄의 용서, 한없는 동정, 불운한 자들에 대한 연민, 하나님과 그의 계획에 대한 강한 믿음이 예수의 살아 있는 유산들이다.

김 시인은 그러한 메시지가 세상에 필요함을 깨닫고 문명의 처방전이라는 시집에서 독창적인 방식과 애정을 담아 그것을 탐색한다. 그의 분노, 슬픔, 두려움과 의심은 모두 우리의 인간성을 일깨우기 위해 펼쳐져 있다. 이것은 시인만이 수용하는 과업이다.

<Review 2> by Duane Vorhees (Dr. Duane Vorhees taught various subjects for the University of Maryland in Korea and Japan before retiring. He now lives in the US and maintains a creative arts site, duanespoetree.blogspot.com. Hawakal recently published his "Love's Autobiography: The Ends of Love.)

I'll build a house of a poem
Because it doesn't have a tyrant's knife
But it can be a teacher
To tame a tyrant's tongue.

I'll build a house of a poem
Because it doesn't have a clever scheme
To prevent time from carving wrinkles on my sweetheart's forehead
But it can be a book to keep forever
Her smiling face.

--from "House of a Poem"

"Prescription of Civilization" is the house that poet Wansoo Kim has constructed. In his preface he recounts his "opportunity to meet God at the revival service of a neighboring church," which led to his composing poems "to express my new insight formed by ... the Christian faith." However, anyone who reads the book expecting a volume of religious verse is likely to be surprised. The first explicitly Christian poem does not appear until the second part of the book, and it is titled "Science."

After the poet has made a global tour of the world's war zones and places of poverty, including the Philippines, Afghanistan, Africa, Iraq, and North Korea, he uses this poem to belittle science as "A monster / with a big head / and so many bright eyes. / But small cold heart // Though you act big pretending to know everything / Always tapping on a calculator / And arranging numbers / Looking into a microscope or telescope, // Aren't you a hardheaded rube? / ... How do you sense the spring water of inspiration / Flowing out of the deep valley of the artist's soul / And shed light on God's providence // That Jesus was born / By the Holy Spirit resting on Mary?"

Once in a while Kim returns to his Christian theme, as in his depiction of an earthworm as "a living transfiguration / Of the person who became the essence of eternal life / Tearing the flesh of his whole body and shedding its blood / After climbing the hill of Cavalry." But more often, as in "An Adopted Son," or "Eyes," or "In the Middle of a Typhoon," his references are less direct and thus open to non-Christian interpretation. Even so, the figure of Jesus inhabits much of his commentary, as in "Christmas Eve," in which he excoriates the expropriation of Biblical feelings for purposes of secularization and monetization. "False Santas / Shake their handbell to open wallets" while "drunken people / Beat on the table with their chopsticks and carols / Chewing Jesus as a side dish."

Kim's other aim as stated in his preface is "to diagnose the disease of modern civilization and find its solution." Again, however, while he attacks self-serving politicians and pens several poems addressing the plight of the Korean peninsula, his suggested solution is essentially humanistic and, especially, is reliant upon artists as cultural pioneers of peace and progress. In discussing Yi Munyol's novel "Our Twisted Hero," he remarks that "it puts the laughing wind / Into the hard and exhausted heart, / ... And it makes the flame of justice / Blaze up in the person blinded by self-interests / And becomes the medium to revive conscience / In the heart of the decaying society."

Aside from Kim's philosophical musings, the real joy of the book's poetry follows familiar Korean natural tropes. The book's first poem depicts the spider's condition: "It gasps entangled / Among the nets / Spun by itself." Elsewhere, the moon is "A woman who has come / Stepping lightly on the darkness / In yellow skirt and coat, / And white socks." Kim's poems also present charming personifications, such as the bag that "knows he won't be filled up / But he always opens his mouth / Just like a man exhausted with hunger."

Although Kim has been writing poetry for more than two decades, this is his first book published for an international audience. Anyone with an interest in the contemporary Korean literary tradition, or in the present world's condition, should find much of interest between its covers.

〈서평2〉 (Duane Vorhees의 Review)

(상략)

시의 집은

폭군의 칼은 없지만

폭군의 혀를 길들이는

스승이 될 수 있으니

시의 집을 지으리

시의 집은

시간이 연인의 이마에

주름살 새기는 걸 막을 묘책은 없지만

연인의 미소 짓는 눈동자를

영원히 간직하는 책이 될 수 있으니

시의 집을 지으리

(하략)

— 〈시의 집〉 부분

　"문명의 처방전"은 김완수 시인이 건축한 시의 집이다. 서문에서 그는 "이웃 교회의 부흥회에서 하나님을 만난 기회"를 상술하는데, 그 일이 "기독교 신앙에 의해 형성된 새로운 통찰력을 표현하는" 시작(詩作)의 동기가 되었다고 한다. 그러나 한 권의 종교시를 기대하며 시집을 읽는 누구도 놀라게 될 것 같다. 최초의 분명한 기독교 신앙시는 시집의 2부, "과학"이라는 제목의 시에서 비로소 등장하기 때문이다.

시인은 1부의 시편들을 통해 필리핀, 아프가니스탄, 아프리카, 이라크, 북한 등을 포함해서 세계의 전쟁 지역과 가난한 곳들을 두루 살핀 후에, 과학(만능주의)의 의미를 축소하기 위해 이 시를 사용한다.

머리는 크고
눈은 많고 밝으나
가슴은 작고 차가운
괴물이여

늘 계산기를 두드리고
현미경이나 망원경을 들여다보며
숫자들을 늘어놓고
모든 것을 다 아는 척 으스대지만

두 영혼이 만나 하나가 되는
사랑이 무엇인지
알지도 느끼지도 못하는
고지식한 풋내기가 아니더냐

그런데도 왜 힘센 독수리처럼 날개를 퍼덕이며
달나라로 날아가
방아 찍는 토끼를 죽여 버리고
별나라로 날아가
견우와 직녀의 사랑을 가로막느냐

네가 어찌 예술가의 영혼 깊은 골짜기에서

흘러나오는 영감의 샘물을 감지하며

마리아에게 성령이 머물러

예수가 태어난

신의 섭리를 밝히겠느냐

— 〈과학〉 전문

이따금 김 시인은 지렁이의 묘사에 있어서와 같이 기독교적 주제로 돌아

간다.

 (상략)

갈보리 언덕을 올라

온몸의 살을 찢고 피를 쏟아

영생(永生)의 진액이 된 자의

살아 있는 변신이다

—〈지렁이〉 부분

그러나 더 자주, 〈양자〉, 〈시선〉, 〈태풍 한가운데서〉 작품에서와 같이,

그의 언급은 덜 직접적이고 비기독교적인 해석에 열려 있다. 그렇기는 하지만,

〈크리스마스 이브〉에서와 같이, 예수라는 인물이 묘사의 많은 곳에 내재되어

있다. 〈크리스마스 이브〉에서, 그는 세속화와 경제적 수익의 목적을 위해 성경적 감정을 수용한 것을 신랄하게 비난한다. "... 취객들이 / 예수를 안주로 씹어대며 / 캐럴에 맞춰 젓가락 장단을 두드리는" 동안, "가짜 산타들이 / 지갑을 열기 위해 방울 종을 흔들고" 있다는 표현이 그러하다.

그의 서문에서 진술된 바와 같이 김 시인의 다른 목적은 "현대 문명의 병폐를 진단하고 그 해결책을 찾는 것"이다. 그러나 다시 그가 이기주의적인 정치가들을 공격하고 한반도의 곤경을 지적하는 수 편의 시를 쓰고 있지만, 그의 암시된 해결책은 본질적으로 인도주의적이고, 특히 평화와 발전의 문화적 개척자로서 예술가를 신뢰하는 태도를 보인다. 이문열의 소설 〈우리들의 일그러진 영웅〉을 논함에 있어서, 그는 다음과 같이 언급한다.

(상략)
힘들고 지친 가슴에
웃음의 바람도 넣어주고
(중략)

사리사욕에 눈먼 자에게
정의의 불길을
타오르게 하고
썩어가는 사회의 가슴에
양심을 되살리는 약이 되기도 하지만
(하략)
　　　― 〈소설, "우리들의 일그러진 영웅"〉 부분

김 시인의 철학적인 사색을 보여주는 시편들 이외에, 이 시집에 수록된 시들 가운데 진정한 기쁨을 주는 것은 친숙한 한국 자연에 대한 비유들이다. 이 시집의 첫 번째 시는 거미의 상태를 이렇게 묘사한다.

(상략)

스스로 푼

실타래에 얽혀

가쁜숨 몰아쉰다

(하략)

      — 〈거미〉 부분

그밖에, 달은 이렇게 묘사된다.

노란 치마저고리

하얀 버선발로

살포시 어둠 딛고

찾아온 여인

(하략)

      — 〈달의 눈물〉 부분

김 시인의 시들은 또한 매력적인 의인법을 보여준다. 예를 들면, 자루를 이렇게 표현한다.

(상략)

차지 않을 걸 알면서도

언제나 허기진 놈처럼

입을 벌린다

(하략)

〈이상한 자루〉 부분

김 시인은 20년 이상 시를 써왔지만, 이것이 국제적인 독자들을 위해 출간되는 첫 번째 시집이다. 현대 한국 문학 전통이나 현재의 세계 상황에 관심이 있는 사람은 누구나 이 시집 안에서 흥미로운 많은 것을 발견하게 될 것이다.

www.ingramcontent.com/pod-product-compliance
Lightning Source LLC
Chambersburg PA
CBHW060803050426
42449CB00008B/1512